Feb - '23

A Special Gift

To: _Anne_

_____

From: _Gr'ma Wedel_

_____

Date: _____

A Mother's Heart

REFLECTIONS
of God's Love

Written by JULIE SUTTON
Illustrated by CONNIE SMILEY

Brownlow

Introduction

Mothers are selfless people. They spend most of their lives caring for others and trying to meet the needs of their children and family. As a result, they spend their days doing countless loads of laundry, driving miles of errands, advising gently the growth of a new adult, and watching hopefully as her children take wing. A mother does all this and more without a ripple of applause. She does it all because it is her nature to love with a love that endures through all. And in this love we see reflections of God's love for His children, for He has promised us that as a mother loves and comforts her child, so He will love and comfort His children.

Why God
Gave Women
Kids...
Reason #387:

They provide the perfect excuse for baking cookies...
ANY time of the month.

Dear Lord,

As I stoop to change a diaper, tie a shoelace or wipe up a sticky mess, may I do it with the humility and gentleness of Jesus, who stooped to heal the leper, feed the hungry, and wash the feet of His disciples.

Some people think of motherhood as boring. I say you've never experienced life on the edge until you've been squirted in the eye by a juice box at 55 mph.

Because you refresh other people, I love you, and I will also refresh you.

PROVERBS 11:25, ADAPTED

Some days a mom has to forget about keeping her dignity and laugh hysterically just to keep her sanity!

Mom's Lament

They pull on my hemline and tug at my sleeve,
They rattle my nerves like you wouldn't believe.
They're noisy, demanding, and grant no reprieve,
These sometimes-impossible children.

I pray for the grace to be loving and kind
As I hear "Mom!" repeated the forty-ninth time!
They hound and annoy, they harass and they whine,
But oh, they adore me, these children.

They ask for the world (and I'm pressed to comply),
They drink up attention and siphon me dry.
I can't always please them, but God knows I try—
He gives me the strength for these children.

I wash dishes and laundry day in and day out,
I'm chauffeur, maid, coach, referee, and Girl Scout!
They're hard to live with—but much harder without,
And how I thank God they're my children!

Can a mother forget the baby at her breast
and have no compassion on the child she has
born? ...I will not forget you!

ISAIAH 49:15

But a mother's love endures through all; in
good repute, in bad repute, in the face of all the
world's condemnation, a mother still loves on,
and still hopes...still she remembers the infant
smiles that once filled her bosom with rapture,
the merry laugh, the joyful shout of his child-
hood, the opening promise of his youth; and she
can never be brought to think him all unworthy.

WASHINGTON IRVING

She is clothed with strength and dignity;
she can laugh at the days to come...

PROVERBS 31:25

Romance fails us—and so
do friendships—but the relationship
of Mother and Child remains
indelible and indestructible—the
strongest bond upon this earth.

THEODOR REIK

My mother's love for me was so great that
I have worked hard to justify it.

MARC CHAGALL

They always looked back before
turning the corner, for their mother
was always at the window to nod
and smile, and wave her hand at them.
Somehow it seemed as if they couldn't
have got through the day without that,
for whatever their mood might be,
the last glimpse of that motherly face
was sure to affect them like sunshine.

LOUISA MAY ALCOTT

When I stopped seeing my mother
with the eyes of a child, I saw the woman
who helped me give birth to myself.

NANCY FRIDAY

Listen, my son, to your father's instruction and do not forsake your mother's teaching. They will be a garland to grace your head and a chain to adorn your neck.

PROVERBS 1:8–9

A mother is not a person to lean on but a person to make leaning unnecessary.

DOROTHY CANFIELD FISHER

I will cover you with my feathers, and under my wings you will find refuge.

PSALM 91:4, ADAPTED

The best advice from my mother was a reminder to tell my children every day: "Remember you are loved."

EVELYN MCCORMICK

A Mother's love gives your heart wings.

Mighty is the force of motherhood!
It transforms all things by its vital heart,
it turns timidity into fierce courage,
and dreadless defiance into tremulous
submission; it turns thoughtlessness
into foresight and yet stills all
self-denial into calm content.

GEORGE ELIOT

The relationship to the mother
is the first and most intense.

SIGMUND FREUD

There never was a woman like her.
She was gentle as a dove
and brave as a lioness.
The memory of my mother and
her teachings were, after all,
the only capital I had
to start life with, and on
that capital I have made my way.

ANDREW JACKSON

The mother!
She is what keeps the family intact.
It is proved. A fact. Time and time again.

ANNA F. TREVISAN

When their children flourish, almost all mothers
have a sense of well-being.

SARA RUDDICK

Through my parents' reading, I learned to love books;
through their philosophy, I learned to think; through
their humor, I learned to laugh…. It was through their
faith that my own was born.

GRACE H. KETTERMAN

By wisdom a house is built, and through
understanding it is established;
through knowledge its rooms are filled
with rare and beautiful treasures.

PROVERBS 24:3–4

The most beautiful flower on earth
grows from the seed of God's love that is planted
in every mother's heart.
MELISSA REAGAN

SEEDS

A woman giving birth to a child has pain
because her time has come; but when her baby
is born she forgets the anguish because
of her joy that a child is born into the world.

JOHN 16:21

Some words are simply not in a mother's vocabulary.
For instance, you never say something is "lost."
Either a) "It's bound to turn up sooner or later,"
b) "It couldn't have just walked away,"
or c) "You'd find it if you cleaned your room."

It's the little things you do day in and day out
that count. That's the way you teach your children.

AMANDA PAYS

The mother's heart is the child's schoolroom.

HENRY WARD BEECHER

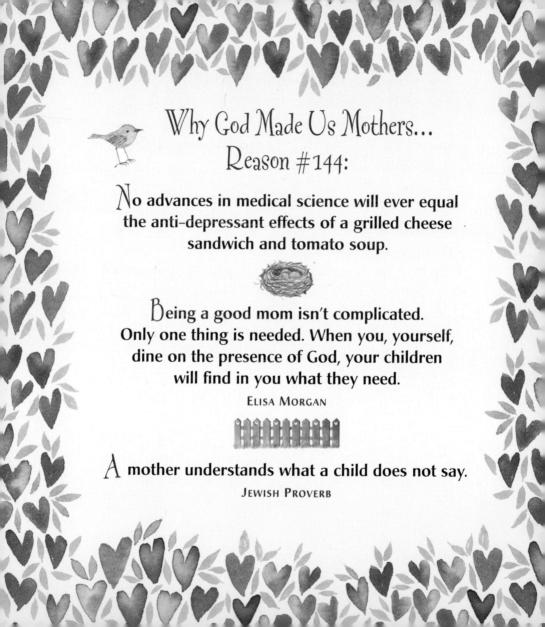

Why God Made Us Mothers...
Reason #144:

No advances in medical science will ever equal the anti-depressant effects of a grilled cheese sandwich and tomato soup.

Being a good mom isn't complicated. Only one thing is needed. When you, yourself, dine on the presence of God, your children will find in you what they need.

ELISA MORGAN

A mother understands what a child does not say.

JEWISH PROVERB

Motherhood–
it's the most work you'll ever do without pay!

No boo-boo can withstand a mother's kiss
and a cool band aid.

MELISSA REAGAN

As a mother loves and comforts her child,
so I will love and comfort you.

ISAIAH 66:13, ADAPTED

None like a mother can charm away pain
From the sick soul and the world-weary brain.

ELIZABETH AKERS ALLEN

Your sons come from afar, and your daughters
are carried on the arm. Then you will look and
be radiant, your heart will throb and swell with joy.

ISAIAH 60:4–5

What is home without a mother?

SEPTIMUS WINNER

There is no love like the good old love—
the love that mother gave us.

EUGENE FIELD

There is no velvet so soft as mother's lap,
no rose so lovely as her smile, no path so flowery
as that imprinted with her footsteps.

ARCHBISHOP THOMSON

Love blooms in a mother's heart.

Mom with a Mission

"Spiderman! Hurry! I need your help.
There are radioactive blobs stuck to the kitchen floor,
and if they aren't removed right away, our entire
family could be destroyed!"

If there's one thing this five-year-old superhero
responds to with enthusiasm, it's being given a
Mission in Life. From our under-the-sink arsenal,
he chooses his weapons: a green sponge along
with a pink plastic scrubber. Last time it was a pair
of makeshift scrub brush "skates" fastened onto his
bare feet with shoelaces. Soon he is busy annihilating
bombs, saving the household from certain death.
Petrified cereal was soaked and pried from their
linoleum minefield; dangerous, sticky Kool-aid spots
are deactivated; sugary deposits under the table are
safely neutralized with our top secret formula
(a mixture of warm water and dish washing liquid).

Even Spiderman's baby brother has joined in the
campaign against evil, as he takes up his own weapon

(a wet rag) against the highly volatile stubborn wall splatters that surround his high chair.

In the next room, Mom blithely wields her feather duster, smug and satisfied, secretly patting herself on the back for her ingenious manipulation of these sometimes-unruly little ones. *How clever I am, she thinks to herself. I've made it all into a game. They're having the time of their lives—and I'm getting my floors scrubbed!*

Meanwhile, up in Heaven, an angel turns to God with an amused countenance. "How did you manage to get her to do your will so easily? Look at her: changing diapers, picking up dirty socks…the same chores that so many women consider drudgery. Yet there she is, grinning and humming to herself as if she couldn't be happier! What did you do?"

"It was nothing," the Lord winks fondly. "After all, it's not hard to motivate someone who has a Mission in Life."

A mother's heart is ever
waiting, and watching,
patiently loving
and teaching
her children.

I am with you every place you go.
I will gently put my hand on you.
My strong right hand will hold you and lead you.

PSALM 139:7–10, ADAPTED

Many years have I sought happiness. I found it first,
perhaps, in the warmth of my mother's breast, and
in the fond caress of her hands, and in the tenderness
that shone in her eyes.

WILL DURANT

Who is it that loves me and will love me forever
with an affection which no chance, no misery,
no crime of mine can do away?
It is you, my mother.

THOMAS CARLYLE

My Mother's Clothes

When I was small, my mother's clothes
All seemed so kind to me!
I hid my face amid the folds
As safe as safe could be.

The gown that she had on
To me seemed shining bright,
For woven in that simple stuff
Were comfort and delight.

Yes, everything she wore
Received my hopes and fears,
And even the garments of her soul
Contained my smiles and tears.

Then softly will I touch
This dress she used to wear.
The old-time comfort lingers yet,
My smiles and tears are there.

A tenderness abides
Though laid so long away,
And I must kiss their empty folds,
So comfortable are they.

ANNA HEMPSTEAD BRANCH

What Happened?

I can't figure out what happened.
Motherhood used to be so simple.
I was full of wisdom, calm and
self-assured, prepared for every situation...
then I had kids.

We do not know what to do,
but our eyes are upon you.

2 CHRONICLES 20:12 (NIV)

Knowing that you release your family in the morning
into the day with your love and with your warmth
is the richness of life.

MARIA SCHELL

All mothers have intuition.
The great ones have radar.

CATHY GUISEWITE

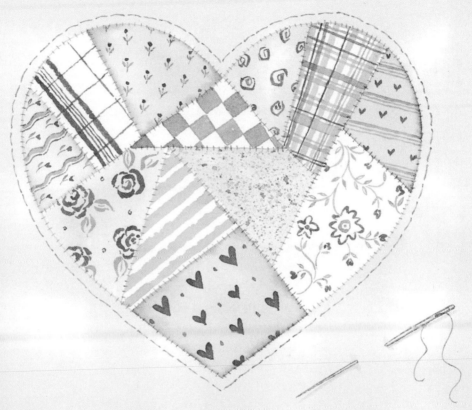

There is no warmth like that of a mother's heart.

A Mother Knows Just What to Do

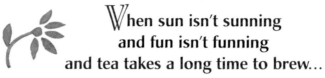

When sun isn't sunning
and fun isn't funning
and tea takes a long time to brew...

When brambles are scratching
or sneezes are catching,
a mother knows just what to do.

If secrets need sharing
or thoughts need comparing,
If life is in slight disarray...

If wee ones need tending
or feelings need mending...
a mother can make life okay!

She'll cuddle and kiss you
and talk through the issue,
and suddenly things are all right...

Her life's such a tizzy
she makes herself dizzy,
but somehow she gets it all done!

She's patient and kind
when her little ones mind—
There's affection in each tender look…

But nothing gets by her—
(Just go on and try her!)—
On mischief, a mom wrote the book!

Ask moms how they do it—
They say, "Nothing to it!"
But everyone knows it's not true.

That's why there's no other
loved more than a mother
who always knows just what to do.

AUTHOR UNKNOWN

a mother holds her children's hands for
a while, their hearts forever. A mother
holds her children's hands for a while, their
hearts forever. A mother holds her childr
hands for a while, their hearts forever. A m
holds her children's hands a while, their
hearts forever. A mother holds her child
hands for a while hearts forever.
A mother holds children's hands f
a while, their hearts forever. Mo
holds her children's hands for a whil

I'm a Child Too

When I look in your eyes…those sweet, trusting eyes
My Father shows me, and I begin to understand,
When I'm holding your hands…those soft, tiny hands
The One who knows me shows me who I really am,
I'm a child too; I'm a child just like you.

And oh, how I need Him; I depend upon Him so
He's watching me closely everywhere I go.

In the middle of the night I awake to hear your cries
And in a moment I'm there to comfort you,
As I'm holding you near and drying all your tears
I know there's Someone who's listening for me too,
I'm a child to Him; I'm a child deep within.

And oh, how He loves me; I am precious in His sight
I call to my Father—He makes everything all right.

And He'll carry me through, just the way I'll carry you
As I see you growing, I'll be growing too,
I'm a child at heart, ready for a brand new start with you.

A Rainbow for You

If I could, I'd write for you a rainbow
And splash it with all the colors of God
And hang it in the window of your being
So that each new morning
Your eyes would open first to Hope and Promise.
If I could, I'd wipe away your tears
And hold you close forever in shalom.
But God never promised
I could write you a rainbow,
Never promised I could suffer for you,
Only promised I could love you.
That I do.

ANN WEEMS

Mother's arms are made of tenderness,
and sweet sleep blesses the child who lies therein.

VICTOR HUGO

Babies are born with a temporary soft spot on their head
as a symbol of the permanent one they are about
to make in your heart.

My mother's hands are cool and fair,
They can do anything.
Delicate mercies hide them there
Like flowers in the spring.

ANNA HEMPSTEAD BRANCH

To a mother there is music
in the tread of childish feet;
In the happy, childish prattle
fraught with laughter gay and sweet...
There is music ev'rywhere,
there is music ev'rywhere,
There is music all around us,
there is music ev'rywhere.

A Mother Understands

When mother sits beside my bed
At night, and strokes and smoothes my head,
And kisses me, I think, some way,
How naughty I have been all day;
Of how I waded in the brook,
And of the cookies that I took,
And how I smashed a window light
A-rassling—me and Bobby White—
And tore my pants, and told a lie;
It almost makes me want to cry
When mother pats and kisses me;
I'm just as sorry as can be,
But I don't tell her so—no, sir.
She knows it all; you can't fool her.

ANONYMOUS

Making the decision
to have a child—
it's momentous.
It is to decide forever
to have your heart
go walking around
outside your body.

ELIZABETH STONE

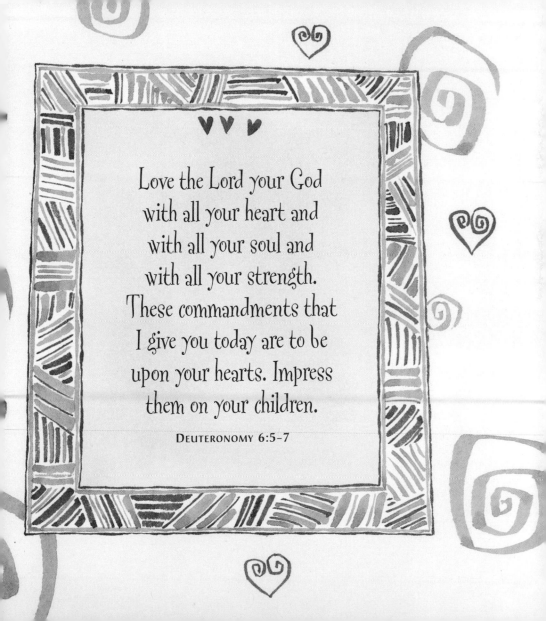

Love the Lord your God
with all your heart and
with all your soul and
with all your strength.
These commandments that
I give you today are to be
upon your hearts. Impress
them on your children.

DEUTERONOMY 6:5-7

Children are God's masterpieces...

Parenting By Numbers

Our first child was raised by the book. Every night I would read the baby books—do this, don't do that—it was rigid. At bath time every night we inspected him for all known communicable diseases—and a few unknown. Every morning we checked little darling to see if he was still breathing.

In retrospect, we were raising a son like painting a picture by numbers. You remember those paint by number pictures, they all have color where they're supposed to, but you know there's something wrong with it. It's too tight, too rigid, too mechanical.

I don't mean to say go soft on the discipline and the training, but we soon decided to parent more by instinct than by the book.

Now that I'm a grandmother, I realize you've got to get good advice as a new mother, but you also have to be yourself. Forget the mechanical, rigid approach, pray for God's help, and begin creating a masterpiece.

CAROLINE BROWNLOW

He tends his flock like a shepherd:
He gathers the lambs in his arms
and carries them close to his heart;
he gently leads those that have young.

ISAIAH 40:11

Some are kissing mothers and some are
scolding mothers, but it is love just the same,
and most mothers kiss and scold together.

PEARL S. BUCK

Blessed are the mothers of the earth,
for they have combined the practical
and the spiritual into one workable
way of human life. They have darned
little stockings, mended little dresses,
washed little faces, and have pointed
little eyes to the stars and little souls
to eternal things.

WILLIAM L. STIDGER